This book belongs to

Nusaybah rauhan

Talukdar y.r 6

Falcons 2022 wed

First published in the United Kingdom in 1428[AH] (2007[CE]) by
Learning Roots Ltd.
Unit 6, TGEC, Town Hall Approach Road
London
N15 4RX
www.learningroots.com

Second edition published in 1432[AH] (2011[CE]).
Reprinted in 1433[AH] (2012[CE]).

Authored by Zaheer Khatri.
Illustrations, typsetting and layout by the Learning Roots Education Design Service.

Acknowledgements
The publisher thanks Allah, Lord of the Worlds, for making this publication possible.

British Library Cataloguing in Publication Data
A CIP catalogue record for this book is available from the British Library

Printed and bound in China.

ISBN: 978-1-905516-17-9

the story of Nuh عليه السلام

*There is instruction in their stories for people of
intelligence. This is not a narration which has been
invented but confirmation of all that came before, a
clarification of everything, and a guidance and a mercy
for people who have iman.*

(The Noble Quran, Surah Yusuf: 111)

contents

You are on a journey.

You will learn about the lives of some of the best men that ever lived.

These were men sent by Allah.

You will learn why they were sent,

who they were sent to,

and what lessons we can learn from their lives.

They are the Prophets.

The first of them is Adam عليه السلام

and the last of them is Muhammad ﷺ.

setting off

As with any journey, you will need to know where you are going; having a map of your route certainly helps! On the following pages you will see a map of the Prophets mentioned in the Noble Quran. Follow the path on the map carefully and look out for the names you have heard before.

From amongst all of these Prophets of Allah, five are mentioned in the Quran (in Surah Al-Ahzaab, Ash-Shura & Al-Ahqaaf) as العزم أولوا or Prophets of great determination. They are Nuh العَلِيْه, Ibrahim العَلِيْه, Musa العَلِيْه, Eesa العَلِيْه and Muhammad ﷺ. The life of Muhammad ﷺ is a whole subject in and of itself. In this series, we'll take a closer look at the other four Prophets mentioned, as well as the Prophet Adam العَلِيْه; the first Prophet of Allah. Take a look at the map on the next page...

Eesa عليه السلام

Ibrahim عليه السلام

Musa عليه السلام

As you may have guessed from the title of this book, you'll be learning about the story of Nuh ﷺ. You can discover more about the other Prophets in the rest of this series.

As you travel, you will need to acquaint yourself with some essential information. Without it, you will be lost, and may not reach your final destination. Read up on the following symbols to find out what to expect along your way.

Before you begin any journey, you need to know where you are going and why you are going there. With all the stories in this book, your aim is broken into three parts. You **must** be able to read the story yourself, summarize the main events and place them in the correct order. You **should** be able to understand the finer details of what occurred in the story. Finally, you **could** be able to understand the reasoning behind some of the story events. You will be able to test whether you have achieved your targets at the end of each section by attempting to overcome the obstacles in your way.

One of the other things you need to do before any journey is to prepare! **Pack Your Bags** involves reminding yourself about the meanings of some essential key words that occur in the story.

Once you have set off on your journey, you'll need to think actively about what you are learning. **Reflections** occur in the middle of stories and get you to ponder a little deeper into the events.

Once the reading is over, you'll take a well earned rest at the **Rest Point**. You'll do some light word-work to ensure you understand the language used in the story.

Now begins your chance to prove what you have learnt. You have to cross three different obstacles, each getting harder as you go along. By completing each of these you will ensure you have covered the aims of your journey. First you have to **Jump the Fence** by proving you know enough about the events of the story.

The next task is a little harder. **Cross the River** is all about checking whether you picked up the smaller details of what actually happened in the story.

The final and hardest task is called **Climb the Mountain.** Here you have to show an understanding of why things happened the way they did in the story.

After completing each section, be sure to have your answers marked in **The Farewell Mark** chapter at the end of this book. Well that's all you need to know before you start! It's time to begin your journey. Bismillah! Here's a little introduction for you…

Allah sent many Prophets after Adam عليه السلام, guiding people to the truth. But Iblees was hard at work too. He hated people praying to Allah alone, so he tricked them into praying to stones. Something had to be done to stop him…

the long call

Before you set off, take a moment to pause and think about the meanings of the words below. You can get a feel for this story just by looking at the words! We'll do some work on them at the end.

WARNING

PROMISE

PUNISHMENT

BELIEVE

Allah sent the Prophet Nuh *'Alay-his-salaam* to guide the people back. It was not an easy thing to do.

"Fear Allah alone and do what Allah likes!" said Nuh.

His people did not want to hear. They just stuck their fingers in their ears and walked away.

"Don't you see how Allah made the moon light up the sky?" said Nuh, "and how He made the sun like a lamp? It was Allah who spread the Earth like a carpet for you. So why don't you give any thanks?"

His people did not care. "You are a man just like us," they said. "We think you are lying."

Only a few people believed with Nuh. The rest of them just turned away. Nuh called them to Allah for nine hundred and fifty years. He never became tired, but his people did.

"You have called us for too long," they said. "If you do not stop, we will stone you!"

The more Nuh called his people, the more they turned away. So Nuh gave them a warning.

"I fear for you the punishment of a painful day," he said.

"Bring us the punishment if you are telling the truth!" said Nuh's people. They had no shame. Now they had gone too far.

Indeed Nuh's عليه السلام people had gone too far! But what exactly is the difference in the way they responded to Nuh عليه السلام before and after his warning? Write your thoughts in the space below and then read on to see if you were right.

....

....

....

....

....

....

....

....

....

....

Allah told Nuh to build a ship. It was all part of Allah's plan. Nuh and the Muslims got to work right away.

But there was no sea nearby for the ship to sail. The people passed by making fun of Nuh. They felt safe from Allah's plan.

"We shall make fun of you," said Nuh, "just like you make fun of us." He believed in the promise of Allah. It was about to come true...

Rest Point

Wondering what will happen next? You'll have to do some work before you can read on. In the spaces provided, write each word in a suitable sentence that shows it's meaning well.

believe

promise

punishment

warning

Muslims

Nuh

share

Jump the Fence

Read the sentences below. Write the letters of the events in the order they occurred in the circles at the bottom of the page. You will have to write the missing events and letters for yourself. What word do the letters spell?

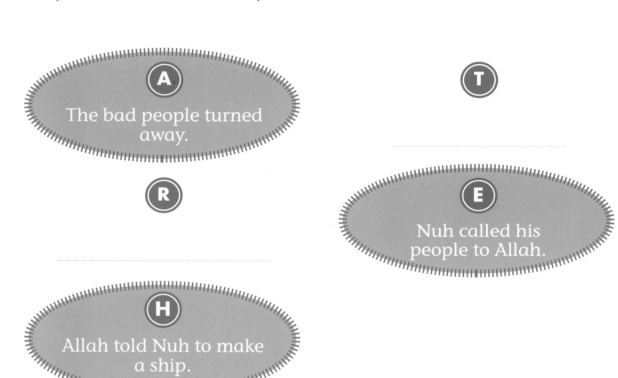

A The bad people turned away.

T

R

E Nuh called his people to Allah.

H Allah told Nuh to make a ship.

Cross the River

We'll make things easy this time by giving you the answers. But wait! You'll have to come up with the questions. Write an appropriate question for each of the following answers in the spaces provided.

1 Nuh told his people to fear Allah and do what Allah likes.

2 Nuh told his people about what Allah had made for them.

3 Nuh's people said they would stone him if he did not stop calling them to Allah.

4 The Muslims helped Nuh build the ship.

5 Nuh warned his people of the punishment of a painful day.

6 Allah told Nuh to build a ship.

7 Nuh told the people that he would make fun of them just as they made fun of him.

8 Nuh called his people to Allah for 950 years.

Climb the Mountain

Time for little table turning! Pair the questions to their answers. The first question has been done for you as an example. Be warned, this is a steep mountain to climb!

Number	1	2	3	4	5	6	7	8
Letter	*f*							

1 A	**2 B**	**3 C**	**4 D**	**5 E**	**6 F**	**7 G**	**8 H**
Why did Allah send the Prophet Nuh?	How can you tell the people didn't listen to Nuh?	Why did the people not care?	Why did the people become tired of Nuh?	Why did Nuh give his people a warning?	How can you tell that the people had no shame?	Why did Allah tell Nuh to build a ship?	Why did the people make fun of Nuh?
They thought Nuh was lying.	It was part of Allah's plan.	The ship was built on dry land.	They turned away the more he called them.	They told Nuh to bring on the punishment.	To call the people back to Allah.	He kept on calling them to Allah for a long time.	They stuck their fingers in their ears.

the high waves

You're about to discover how this story will end. Perhaps the words below may give you some idea about what will happen next. See if you know what they mean before you set off. As ever, we'll do some work on these and other words at the end of the story.

GUSHED

SPROUTING

DROWNED

SWALLOWED

Nuh boarded the ship with the Muslims. They began in the name of Allah. *Bismillah!* Animals of every kind came too. They came flying, hopping and jumping in pairs.

The rest of the people stayed behind. They thought it was all a joke. There was no turning back now.

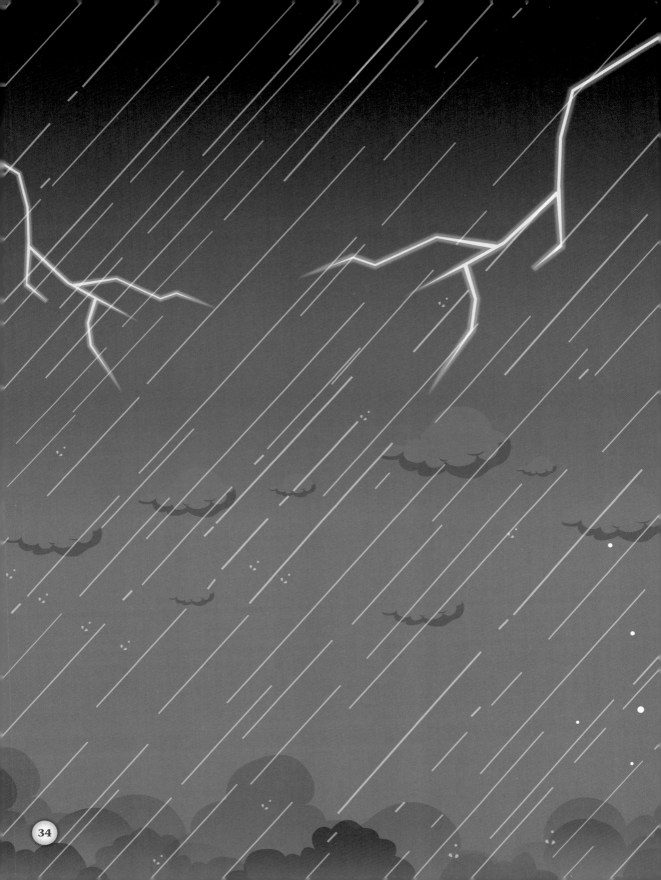

So you're on the brink of finding out what really happens next! Well there are plenty of clues. One of them is the animals that came on board the ship. What clue do you think this gives and why? Write your thoughts in the space below, then turn over to see if you were right in your thinking.

Suddenly, rain poured down from the sky. Water gushed from springs sprouting in the ground. Sea waves rose like mountains. Water was flowing everywhere.

Riding high on the waves, the ship was safe. The people on the ground found no place to hide. The tides swept them away. They drowned and were never seen again.

The Earth swallowed the water and the sky stopped its rain. The ship landed on a mountain. Nuh and the Muslims were safe.

Shaytaan's trick did not work with Nuh. He followed the truth and did what Allah likes. That is our aim in life.

Rest Point

What an ending! But our work is not done yet. Write each word below in a suitable sentence, and provide meanings of the words where asked.

suddenly

Meaning

Sentence

springs

Meaning

Sentence

sprouting

Sentence

Sentence

gushed

Sentence

drowned

Sentence

tides

swallowed

Sentence

Sentence

swept

Jump the Fence

Below is a summary of the main events of the story, but the events are in the wrong order. Read the summary and then rewrite it with the events in the correct order as they occurred in the story.

The bad people were washed away. The ship was safe on the high waves. Nuh boarded the ship with the Muslims. Allah saved Nuh and the Muslims. Water fell from the sky and the sea waves rose very high.

Cross the River

Now let's cross the river. For each question, select one correct answer from the list of five possible answers. Write the letters for each of your answers in order in the shapes below. What word do they spell?

What did Nuh say when he boarded the ship?

Y La ilaaha illallah

Z Alhamdulillah

A Assalaamu-'alaykum

B Bismillah

C Allah-u-Akbar

Who else boarded the ship with Nuh?

N The bad people.

O The Muslims.

P The weak people.

Q Those who could not swim.

R The strong people.

Describe how the animals came on board the ship?

W	*In groups of five.*
X	*One by one.*
Y	*In groups of three.*
Z	*In groups of four.*
A	*In pairs.*

Who stayed behind?

R	*The bad people.*
S	*The Muslims.*
T	*The animals.*
U	*The strong people.*
V	*Nuh.*

Where did all the water begin to come from?

B	*From the earth but not from the sky.*
C	*From the sky but not from the earth.*
D	*From the sky and from the earth.*
E	*From the water taps.*
F	*From the mountains.*

Where was the only safe place?

F   *The ground.*

G   *The mountains.*

H   *The trees.*

I   *The ship.*

J   *The caves.*

What happened to the people on the ground?

N   *They were washed away and died.*

O   *They were washed away but did not die.*

P   *They hid in caves and were saved.*

Q   *They climbed high mountains and were saved*

R   *They climbed tall trees and were saved.*

How did the water go away?

D   *The water evaporated.*

E   *The earth swallowed the water, but it kept on raining.*

F   *It stopped raining, but the earth did not swallow the water.*

G   *The earth swallowed the water and the sky stopped its rain.*

H   *The water flowed into the sea.*

Climb the Mountain

There are just four more questions to complete. Correct the statements in the boxes below.

1

It was all a big test because the bad people were saved in the end.

2

The ship came down to the ground because there was a hole in it.

3

The ship was safe because it sunk in the sea.

4

The bad people stayed behind because they thoguht it was all real.

the farewell mark

Every journey, no matter how long, must come to an end. You have come to the end of your journey through the life of Nuh ﷺ. One of the ways you can measure your success is through seeing how well you did in clearing the obstacles that came in your path. Suggested answers to each chapter are offered in the pages that follow. You are encouraged to have your progress marked.

However, there is more to measuring your success than just clearing the obstacles. One of the most valuable measures is your own thoughts on what you have learnt and enjoyed most. Hopefully, you will take away a treasure chest of lessons from this wonderful and important story, and continue learning more about it in the future. This chapter offers you the chance to judge for yourself what was your most valuable farewell mark.

At the end of a journey, it's always nice to pause and think over what you can most benefit from. Think hard about what were the most valuable lessons you learnt during this journey. Take a moment to think again and select one lesson, idea or thought that you will take away from your experience...

Did you really think
it was all over?

Some time went by, but Shaytaan did not rest. People fell for his tricks again. They carved shapes from stones and prayed to them. It seems as thought they never learned. Did they really want to be taught the lesson again?

Discover what happens in the story of Ibrahim ﷺ.

the long call

Section	Answer	Comments
	Before, Nuh's people did not believe him, but now they were asking for the punishment to be brought onto themselves.	
	Believe: Nuh believed in the promise of Allah. **Promise:** Allah's promise for the believers who do good deeds is Paradise. **Punishment:** Nuh's people asked for the punishment to be brought onto themselves. **Warning:** Nuh gave his people a warning about the punishment of a painful day. **Muslims:** The Muslims took their way with Nuh. **Nuh:** Nuh was the Prophet of Allah. **Share:** Muslims had to share the ship with animals of every kind.	*The answers offered here are by way of suggestion only. Credit should be given for any valid response.*
	E: Nuh called his people to Allah. **A:** The bad people turned away. **R:** Nuh told them about the punishment of a painful day. **T:** The bad people asked Nuh to bring the punishment on. **H:** Allah told Nuh to make a ship. **Word spelt:** EARTH	
	1. What did Nuh tell the people to do? **2.** What did Nuh tell his people about? **3.** What did the people say they would do to Nuh if he did not stop calling them to Islam? **4.** Who helped Nuh build the ship? **5.** What was the warning that Nuh gave to his people? **6.** What did Allah tell Nuh to build? **7.** What did Nuh tell the people when they made fun of him for building the ship? **8.** How long did Nuh call his people to Allah for?	
	1F • 2H • 3A • 4G • 5D • 6E • 7B • 8C	

the high waves

Section	Answer	Comments
	The animals were moved off the ground into the safety of the ship. This shows that anyone left on the ground would not be not safe from the punishment that was about to come.	
	Suddenly: Without warning. **Springs:** Outlet of water source from the ground. **Sprouting:** Weeds began sprouting around everywhere on the ground. **Gushed:** The springs gushed with water. **Drowned:** Those who did not go on the ship where drowned in the water. **Tides:** Big tides in the sea swept the people away. **Swallowed:** The man swallowed his medicine in one go. **Swept:** The man swept the floor clean.	*The answers offered here are by way of suggestion only. Credit should be given for any valid response.*
	Nuh boarded the ship with the Muslims. Water fell from the sky and the sea waves rose very high. The ship was safe on the high waves. The bad people were washed away. Allah saved Nuh and the Muslims.	
	Word spelt: BOARDING	
	1. It was all a big test to see if the people would put their trust in Allah and follow the truth. **2.** The ship came down to the ground because all the water left. **3.** The ship was safe because it rode the waves by the will of Allah. **4.** The bad people stayed behind because they thought it was all a joke.	*The answers offered here are by way of suggestion only. Credit should be given for any valid response.*